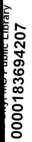

STEM IN THE REAL WORLD

MATHEMATICS
IN THE REAL WORLD

by Christine Zuchora-Walske

Content Consultant
Dr. Karin Wiburg
Professor of Learning Technologies
New Mexico State University

Core Library

An Imprint of Abdo Publishing
abdopublishing.com

abdopublishing.com

Published by Abdo Publishing, a division of ABDO, PO Box 398166, Minneapolis, Minnesota 55439. Copyright © 2016 by Abdo Consulting Group, Inc. International copyrights reserved in all countries. No part of this book may be reproduced in any form without written permission from the publisher. Core Library™ is a trademark and logo of Abdo Publishing.

Printed in the United States of America, North Mankato, Minnesota
082015
012016

THIS BOOK CONTAINS RECYCLED MATERIALS

Cover Photo: iStockphoto
Interior Photos: iStockphoto, 1, 11, 17, 20, 39, 43; Universal History Archive/UIG/Getty Images, 4; NASA, 7, 8, 34; Mauricio Anton/Science Source, 14; Red Line Editorial, 19, 31; Oxford Science Archive/Print Collector/Getty Images, 23; Universal History Archive/Getty Images, 26; Charles Krupa/AP Images, 28, 45; Torin Halsey/Wichita Falls Times Record News/AP Images, 32; Jens Meyer/AP Images, 36; Jim Fitzgerald/AP Images, 40

Editor: Arnold Ringstad
Series Designer: Ryan Gale

Library of Congress Control Number: 2015945540

Cataloging-in-Publication Data
Zuchora-Walske, Christine
Mathematics in the real world / Christine Zuchora-Walske
    p. cm. -- (STEM in the real world)
ISBN 978-1-68078-041-3 (lib. bdg.)
Includes bibliographical references and index.
1. Mathematics--Juvenile literature.   I. Title.
510--dc23

                                                                    2015945540

CONTENTS

CHAPTER ONE

THE POWER OF MATHEMATICS

In 1781 a brother and sister in England found something amazing. William and Caroline Herschel discovered a new planet. It was the first planet found with a telescope. William and Caroline had built the telescope themselves.

Until then, there were only six known planets. They were Mercury, Venus, Earth, Mars, Jupiter, and

The Herschels' discovery launched a race to find more planets. Math was a key tool in this race.

Saturn. Suddenly the solar system was bigger. People realized it might contain more than they knew.

Expanding the Solar System

Scholars named the seventh planet after the Greek god Uranus. Soon many scientists were studying the new planet. They recorded its movements. They used math to figure out its orbit. This is the path a planet takes around the sun. Astronomers could predict where Uranus would appear in the future.

But the numbers were not lining up. Scientists kept finding Uranus not quite where they expected it to be. It had a bit of a wobble in its orbit. They knew the gravity of the sun and planets was not causing this.

Gravity

Every object pulls on every other object. This force is called gravity. The amount of pull an object has depends on its mass. The more mass it has, the harder it pulls. And the closer two objects are, the stronger the pull. Gravity weakens quickly as the distance between objects grows. In the late 1600s, English scientist Isaac Newton described gravity using math.

The movement of Uranus suggested yet another planet lay beyond it.

Neptune is approximately 1 billion miles (1.6 billion km) further from the sun than Uranus.

In 1841 John Couch Adams set out to solve the puzzle. He was an English astronomy student. Adams thought another planet lay beyond Uranus. This new planet's gravity might be causing the wobble. Adams used math to figure out where the mystery planet should be. Meanwhile, French scientist Urbain Le Verrier was doing the same thing.

Adams and Le Verrier both calculated the mystery planet's orbit. They did it within days of each other. But Le Verrier had better luck finding a professional astronomer. He wrote about his calculation to German astronomer Johann Galle. Five days later, Galle received the letter and began searching. He found the mystery planet within 30 minutes. It was soon named Neptune.

The discovery of Neptune was important for two reasons. First, it expanded our understanding of the solar system once again. Second, it showed the amazing power of math. Calculations led directly to a real-life discovery. And it was no small discovery.

It was a huge planet millions of miles away.

Understanding the Universe

Math is so powerful it can find planets. It can also do much more. People have used math for everything from counting objects to measuring the universe.

Math is the study of quantities. Its main tools are numbers. Math involves understanding numbers and the relationships between them. It is also the study of shapes and patterns in nature. Math helps us describe the universe.

Workers called surveyors use numbers, math, and tools to describe landscapes.

Math is a broad field of study. It reaches into every other field. People study and use numbers in many different ways. Math can be divided into several major branches. Arithmetic is adding, subtracting, multiplying, and dividing numbers. Number theory is the study of whole numbers. Geometry is the study of lines, shapes, and angles. Applied math is using math to solve problems in other fields.

Math plays a role in every career. Air traffic controllers use it to plan the paths of airplanes. Animators use math to create the illusion of movement. Architects use math to design safe and useful buildings. Math has made our modern world possible. It has changed the course of history. It continues to do so today.

John Adams Couch wrote the following about the studies of Uranus's unusual orbital motion:

> *I find among my papers the following memorandum, dated July 3, 1841: "Formed a design . . . of investigating . . . the irregularities in the motion of Uranus, which are yet unaccounted for, in order to find whether they may be attributed to the action of an undiscovered planet beyond it, and, if possible, thence to determine approximately the elements of its orbit, etc., which would probably lead to its discovery."*

Source: *"John Couch Adams' Account of the Discovery of Neptune."* History of Mathematics Archive. *University of St. Andrews, March 2006. Web. Accessed July 27, 2015.*

Consider Your Audience

Review this passage closely. It was published in 1847, when scientists used different terms than modern scientists do. For example, Couch used the term *design* where we would say *plan*. Consider how you would rewrite this passage for a modern audience, such as your parents or younger friends. Write a blog post telling this same information to the new audience. How does your new approach differ from the original text, and why?

CHAPTER TWO

THE HISTORY OF MATH

Humans have always thought about math. Amounts, sizes, shapes, and speed are key to surviving. Early humans had to notice when food was scarce. They had to judge how far away prey was. They had to do the same for dangerous animals.

Humans are born with basic math abilities. But they are not born knowing how to do complex math.

Prehistoric people used basic math and numbers for survival.

Tally Marks versus Symbols

When you tally, you make one mark for each item you are counting. You record one item with one mark, ten items with ten marks, and so on. In a symbolic number system, each amount has a different symbol. For example, you record one item with the symbol standing for 1 and ten items with the symbol standing for 10.

That knowledge takes experience, effort, and time. It took thousands of years for people to develop modern math.

The Evolution of Math Concepts

It is one thing to see the difference between one lion and ten. This is an example of concrete thinking. It is another thing to express this idea with words or symbols. This is abstract thinking. Early people lived mainly by hunting animals and gathering plants. They found little need for abstract math.

But over time, people settled down. They grew crops. They raised animals. They began storing food and other goods. They traded with one another. These lifestyle changes sparked a change in math.

Today's farmers continue to use math when working with their crops.

People began using numbers in more abstract ways. They measured their land. They kept track of property. They recorded trade. They noted the movement of objects in the night sky.

The earliest evidence of abstract math thinking comes from approximately 20,000 years ago. Archeologists have found animal bones from that era in east-central Africa. The bones are carved with rows of notches. Scientists think these bones might show a number system. Some think they might even be calendars.

Counting by tally marks led to symbolic number systems. One system appeared in Sumer, located in modern Iraq, around 3000 BCE. At first the Sumerians used clay tokens to represent property. When someone gained or lost property, an official added or subtracted tokens.

By approximately 1700 BCE, Sumer gave way to Babylon. Babylonians pressed tokens into clay to create symbols. They gave different values to different

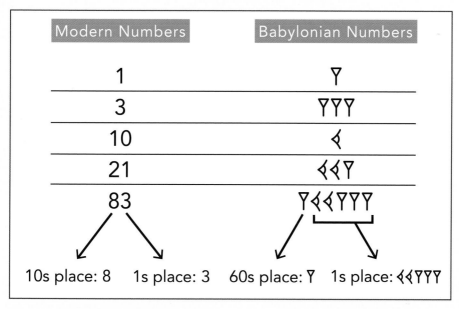

Modern Numbers	Babylonian Numbers
1	𒁹
3	𒁹𒁹𒁹
10	𒌋
21	𒌋𒌋𒁹
83	𒁹𒌋𒌋𒁹𒁹𒁹

10s place: 8   1s place: 3   60s place: 𒁹   1s place: 𒌋𒌋𒁹𒁹𒁹

Base-Ten and Base-Sixty

The modern number system is base-ten. Its place values are the 1s place, the 10s place, the 100s place, and so on. Babylonian place values are the 1s place, the 60s place, the 3600s place, and so on. In this table, you can see how the same amount (83) is written differently using the two number systems.

symbols. These symbols were the first written numbers. Babylonian number symbols went up to sixty. Each amount up to sixty had a different symbol. All Babylonian numbers were made of combinations of those sixty symbols. They used what is called a base-sixty system.

Babylonians came up with an important math idea. This was the use of zero as a placeholder.

The ancient Greek thinker Euclid is often called the "father of geometry."

The Babylonians needed a symbol to show the idea of no amount in a certain place value. For example, the zero in the number 102 means there are no tens. Without a zero, people might misread it as 12.

The ancient Greeks borrowed many math ideas from the Babylonians. They used a base-ten number system from the ancient Egyptians. They also came up with new ideas. Greek scholars created the field of geometry.

These are just a few of the math concepts invented in ancient times. Ideas people take for granted today developed over a long time. The progress of mathematics has sped up dramatically in the last few centuries. Much of this progress was triggered by the use of applied math. People began combining math and science to describe our universe.

Applied Math

Math has helped humans make many useful discoveries. For example, at one time most people believed Earth was the center of the universe.

They could see the sun, moon, and stars crossing the sky. It seemed obvious that they were circling the Earth.

It took two centuries of effort to prove this wrong. In the early 1500s, Polish scholar Nicolaus Copernicus studied the night sky. The motions he saw did not match well with the geocentric, or Earth-centered, rules he had learned. He used math to create a new model of the solar system. His model had the sun at its center. The planets orbited the sun in circles. In the early 1600s, German mathematician Johannes Kepler studied astronomy measurements. He looked at the most complete and accurate data available. Kepler decided Copernicus was mostly correct. However, Kepler showed that the planets orbited in ovals rather than in circles.

Around this time, the telescope was invented. Italian mathematician Galileo Galilei turned his telescope toward the sky. He observed Earth's moon and moons orbiting Jupiter. Galileo was briefly put

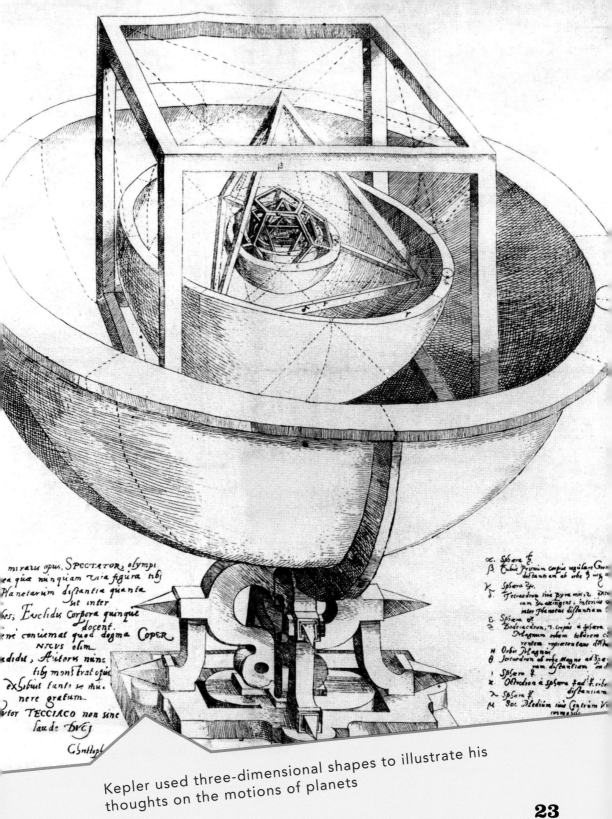

Kepler used three-dimensional shapes to illustrate his thoughts on the motions of planets

23

under house arrest. This was punishment for saying Earth was not the center of the universe. Religious authorities of his time said everything revolved around the Earth. Galileo's observations contradicted this. He later kept his ideas quiet. Finally, in the late 1600s, English mathematician Isaac Newton tied together the work of Copernicus, Kepler, and Galileo. Newton used math to show that the laws of motion in space and those on Earth were the same. He showed that gravity is what keeps the planets circling the sun. Once again, math had changed human ideas about the universe.

Computing

The computer is another useful result of applied math. Computers grew from the need to count and calculate large numbers. The earliest counting tool appeared in the 2000s BCE. It was the counting board. This tool was a wood, clay, stone, or metal tablet. It had a slot for each place value. Counters such as pebbles were used in each slot.

In the early 1600s, people began making mechanical calculators. These calculators worked with gears, like wind-up clocks. In the early 1800s, Englishman Charles Babbage came up with the idea of running a mechanical calculator with a steam engine. He worked with Ada Lovelace, a mathematician who developed ways to use his calculating device. Then, in the 1880s, American engineer Herman Hollerith designed an electric mechanical calculator. This machine worked so well

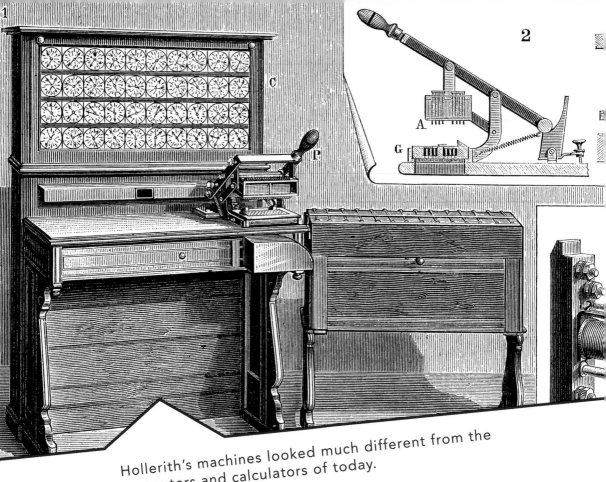

Hollerith's machines looked much different from the computers and calculators of today.

Hollerith started his own calculator business. That company became International Business Machines (IBM). It still exists today. Modern computers do much more than arithmetic. But their origins lie in the need for quicker calculations.

In 1889 Herman Hollerith wrote about the difficulties of completing a census, the measurement of a country's population, by hand:

> *Although our population is constantly increasing, and although at each census more complicated combinations and greater detail are required in the various compilations, still, up to the present time, substantially the original method of compilation has been employed; that of making tally-marks in small squares and then adding and counting such tally-marks. . . . While engaged in work upon the tenth census, the writer's attention was called to the methods employed in the tabulation of population statistics and the enormous expense involved. These methods were at the time described as "barbarous, some machine ought to be devised for the purpose of facilitating such tabulations."*
>
> Source: Herman Hollerith. "An Electric Tabulating System." Columbia University Computing History. *Columbia University, n.d. Web. Accessed July 27, 2015.*

What's the Big Idea?

In this passage the author, Herman Hollerith, describes why he designed an electric calculating machine for the 1890 US Census. Read the text carefully and figure out its main idea. Next, explain how the main idea is supported by details. What are two or three of those supporting details?

CHAPTER THREE

MAKING A LIVING WITH MATH

When hearing the word *mathematician*, some may picture a college professor. Others may imagine an accountant. Many mathematicians work in education. And it is true that accountants need good math skills. But those are just two ways people use math to make a living. There are many career fields that involve mathematics.

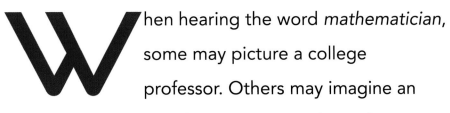

Becoming a math professor is one of many career options in mathematics.

Math Research

Research mathematicians usually work at universities. They study unexplained problems in known mathematics. These thinkers are on the cutting edge of math knowledge. They have doctoral degrees, or PhDs, in math. They often spend part of their time teaching math to college students. The rest of their time is spent on research. Some mathematicians also work with educators to improve how math is taught in schools.

Animator

An animator creates art that looks as if it is moving. He or she makes many pictures, called frames. The frames are shown quickly to create the illusion of motion. Animation appears in movies, on television shows, and on the Internet. Animators use geometry to figure out how objects change shape as they move.

Architect

An architect designs buildings. He or she makes drawings. The drawings show every part of the building. This includes parts hidden from view. Wiring, air conditioning, and plumbing are all planned out.

Career	Approximate Starting Salary
Petroleum Engineering	$102,000
Chemical Engineering	$70,000
Computer Engineering	$67,000
Nuclear Engineering	$67,000
Electrical Engineering	$66,000
Aerospace Engineering	$65,000
Electronics & Communications Engineering	$64,000
Actuarial Mathematics	$61,000

The Payoff

Math is useful and fascinating. And a career in math can really pay off. Many of today's highest-paying careers involve math. This chart shows several of these careers, along with typical starting pay. How does math figure into each of these jobs? What other math-related jobs can you think of?

Architects use math to ensure buildings are safe and useful. Math helps architects spot challenges and find solutions. It helps them design spaces that are pleasant and practical.

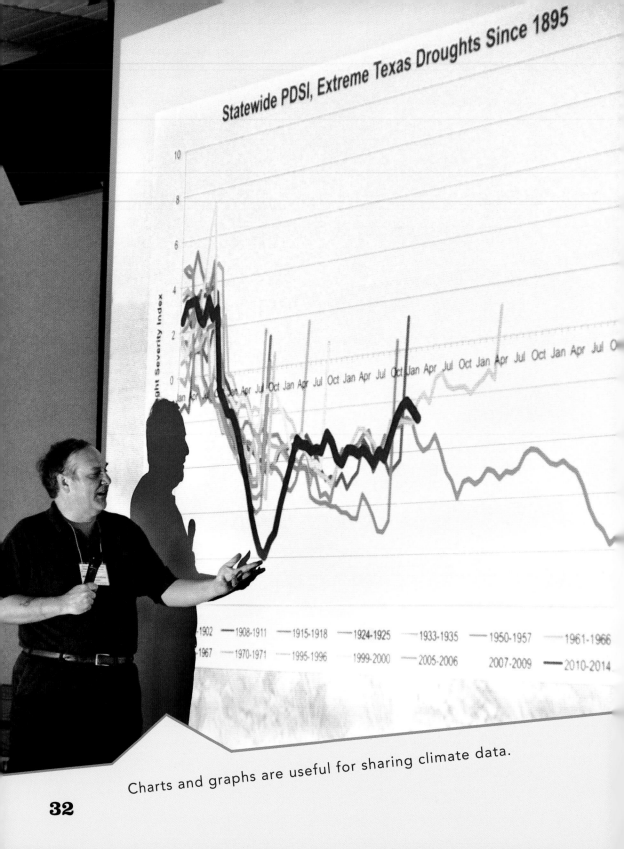

Charts and graphs are useful for sharing climate data.

Climatologist

A climatologist studies weather patterns over time. He or she uses past patterns to help predict the future climate. Climatologists use math to collect weather data, analyze it, and make predictions. They design and use complex computer programs. These programs describe changes in Earth's atmosphere using math.

Forensic Analyst

A forensic analyst is a scientist who helps solve crimes. He or she studies evidence from a crime to

IN THE REAL WORLD
Math in Action

Robert Stewart was an air force test pilot, a NASA engineer, and a space shuttle astronaut. These jobs brought math vividly to life for him. As a test pilot, he found that "the ultimate test of a mathematical analysis is to bet your life on it." As an engineer, he learned "it was harder to bet someone else's life on a mathematical analysis than it was to bet my own." As a shuttle astronaut, Stewart found joy in math: "Being all alone [in space] makes one very happy that Isaac Newton and Johannes Kepler were steadfast in their pursuit of mathematics."

Getting astronauts to space and to the moon requires lots of complex math.

find clues about what happened. Forensic analysts use math to analyze blood, match fingerprints, and study human tissues. They also use math to study video recordings, documents, and traces of chemicals.

Market Researcher

A market researcher gathers information about the economy. He or she helps companies understand what people want and how much they will pay. Market researchers use math to study past sales. They use this information to predict future sales. They also study competing companies.

And More

These math careers are just a few examples. Math is also vital to engineers, programmers, lawyers, military officers, and many other types of people. Many careers that are directly related to math require a college degree in math or a related field.

EXPLORE ONLINE

Chapter Three describes many math-related careers. The website below offers profiles of real people who are working in these careers. How is the information from the website the same as the information in Chapter Three? What new information did you learn from the website?

Mathematical Association of America: Career Profiles

mycorelibrary.com/mathematics

CHAPTER FOUR

TOMORROW'S MATHEMATICS

**W**hat will math look like in the future? This may seem like a strange question. After all, math doesn't change. One plus one is always two. A triangle always has three sides. Tomorrow's math may seem like it will be the same as today's.

This is partially true, but it is not the end of the story. The ideas people know and use today will

Today's mathematicians use huge supercomputers to make new discoveries.

Improving Math: Pi

The number pi is represented by the symbol π. It is one of the most fascinating numbers. It represents the ratio of a circle's circumference to its diameter. Pi is equal to approximately 3.14. Pi is an irrational number, meaning its digits continue forever after the decimal point. People have been trying to calculate more of these digits for thousands of years. By 1400 pi had been calculated to ten decimal places. By 1700 mathematicians had calculated it to more than 100 places. In 2014 researchers calculated pi to more than 13 trillion decimal places.

still exist tomorrow. But people will also come up with new ideas. They will build on the familiar old ones.

Changes and Challenges

Even though much of mathematics will remain the same, many people agree math education has to change. Students will need to learn and use math differently in the future.

In the past, math has mostly been about knowing the right symbols and formulas. It has been about being able to do

Mathematicians believe students must learn how math works, rather than just memorizing formulas.

calculations that solve specific problems. But the world is changing fast. People are building faster and faster computers. As computers grow more powerful, more common, and easier to use, they manage these calculations for us.

Students will need to know not only the math but also the reasons why math works. They will need to experience how math plays out in real life. This will

Computers, tablets, and other technology tools are becoming important parts of modern math classes.

help them understand the basic ideas that serve as building blocks of math. With a deep understanding of basic math ideas, today's students will not be limited to simply following checklists and rules. Instead they will be able to think mathematically. This will help them solve the problems of tomorrow.

FURTHER EVIDENCE

Reread this chapter and identify its main point. List the key evidence you see to support that point. Then read the news article below. Find a quote in the news article that supports the chapter's main point. Does the news quote support a piece of evidence you found in the chapter or add a new one?

Real-World Math

mycorelibrary.com/mathematics

- Ancient people developed the earliest forms of math to help them trade and farm.

- The ancient Greeks, Sumerians, and Babylonians created mathematical concepts we still use today.

- Math plays a big role in everyday life.

- Math is a very broad field of study that reaches into every other field of study.

- Math includes many branches, including arithmetic, geometry, number theory, and applied math.

- Applied math is using math to solve real-world problems.

- All science careers require good math skills.

- All math-related careers require a two-year or four-year college degree.

- Tomorrow's mathematicians must know how to think mathematically, not just follow the rules of math.

Why Do I Care?

Can you think of two or three ways that math is at work in your life? For example, have you followed a recipe? Have you had to double or triple a recipe for a large group? Have you earned money and added it to your savings? Have you gone shopping? Have you built a fort or decorated your room? Have you flipped a coin? How was math involved in each of these activities?

You Are There

Imagine you are a mathematician studying a newly discovered object in space. You are recording its location every day. You are using math to find out if, how, where, and how fast it is moving. Write 200 words describing your observations and your work. How do you gather information? How do you work with other scientists? What questions are you asking?

Say What?

Studying math can mean learning a lot of new vocabulary. Find five words in this book you've never heard before. Use a dictionary to find out what they mean. Then write the meanings in your own words, and use each word in a new sentence.

Surprise Me

Chapter Two discusses events in the history of math. After reading this chapter, what two or three facts about math history did you find most surprising? Write a few sentences about each fact. Why did you find each fact surprising?

GLOSSARY

abstract
expressing a quality or idea
without reference to an
actual person or thing

analyze
to study or find out the
nature of something and
relationship of its parts

arithmetic
adding, subtracting,
multiplying, and dividing
numbers

concrete
based on an actual
experience, person, or thing

formula
a general fact or rule
expressed in mathematical
symbols

geometry
the study of points, lines,
angles, surfaces, and solids

gravity
a force of attraction between
particles or bodies that
occurs because of their mass

number theory
the study of positive whole
numbers (1, 2, 3, 4, and so
on) and the relationships
among them

place value
the value of the location of a
digit in a number

whole number
a number that has no decimal
places or fractions

LEARN MORE

Books

Ball, Johnny. *Go Figure! A Totally Cool Book about Numbers.* New York: DK Publishing, 2005.

Goldsmith, Mike. *How to Be a Math Genius.* New York: DK Publishing, 2012.

Tahan, Malba. *The Man Who Counted: A Collection of Mathematical Adventures.* New York: W. W. Norton, 2015.

Websites

To learn more about STEM in the Real World, visit **booklinks.abdopublishing.com**. These links are routinely monitored and updated to provide the most current information available.

Visit **mycorelibrary.com** for free additional tools for teachers and students.

INDEX

ABOUT THE AUTHOR

Christine Zuchora-Walske has been writing and editing children's books and articles for more than twenty years. She writes about science, history, and current events. Christine lives in Minneapolis with her husband and two children.